What did Jesus do?

What did Jesus do?

A ten-week look at what
Jesus said and did

Suzi Stock

**kevin
mayhew**

Acknowledgements

The publishers wish to express their gratitude to the following copyright holders who have granted permission to include their material in this book:

Wayne Rice, *More Hot Illustrations for Youth Talks.* © Copyright 1995 by Youth Specialities Inc. Used by permission of The Zondervan Corporation, Zondervan 5300 Patterson SE, Grand Rapids, MI 49530, USA.

Michael Puffett and Sheldon Rottler, *Red Hot Ice-Breakers.* © Copyright Monarch Books, Concorde House, Grenville Place, Mill Hill, London NW7 3SA

Every effort has been made to trace the owners of copyright material, and we hope that no copyright has been infringed. Pardon is sought and apology made if the contrary be the case, and a correction will be made in any reprint of this book.

First published in 2004 by

KEVIN MAYHEW LTD
Buxhall, Stowmarket, Suffolk, IP14 3BW
E-mail: info@kevinmayhewltd.com

KINGSGATE PUBLISHING INC
1000 Pannell Street, Suite G, Columbia, MO 65201
E-mail: sales@kingsgatepublishing.com

9 8 7 6 5 4 3 2 1 0

ISBN 1 84417 220 1
Catalogue No 1500693

Cover design by Jonathan Stroulger
Edited by Katherine Laidler
Typesetting by Louise Selfe

Printed and bound in Great Britain

Contents

(These sessions can be run in any order.)

Introduction

Many Christians wear the famous 'WWJD' bracelets intended to remind them of what Jesus would do in the day-to-day situations they are faced with. As much as I support this principle, it only works if we know what Jesus actually did!

This tried and tested resource is designed to introduce young people to what Jesus did and said, in order to help them know what to do. It looks at various topics most young people are faced with and then explores what Jesus did in similar situations, or what he said.

Hopefully, by learning about what Jesus did and said, young people will be equipped to ask what would Jesus do and therefore be able to live a life pleasing to God.

This resource comprises ten sessions. Each session uses icebreaker games, video clips, Bible talks, group discussion and prayer. By breaking it up like this different people can lead each part. It is simple and to the point and can be adapted to all kinds of youth groups. All the films mentioned in this resource can be hired from most good video stores.

I hope *What did Jesus do?* introduces many more young people to the basic principles of our faith and most importantly to their Lord and Saviour.

Suzi Stock

Week 1
Nagging parents!

① Icebreaker

• Spanish Inquisition

Choose a few couples to play this game in front of everybody. The game begins with the first person asking the second person a question. The second person has to answer the first person with a 'logical' question following on from the first and so on. The loser is the first person to give a straight answer.

For example:
'Where have you been all this time?'
'Why do you want to know?'
'Don't you think I have the right to know?'

prize for pairs who get up to 20Q.

② • Can you follow instructions? (See page 11.)

Give out the instructions to each person and when everyone has finished see what is on people's bits of paper.

So often the problem with parents is that we do not understand them and they do not understand us. We fail to communicate – neither of us listens properly and neither of us shares properly. Communication is a two-way thing.

Video clip

Play a clip from *Billy Elliott* where Billy's father finds out he has been having ballet classes. The clip is 21min 56sec from the start and runs for 6min 12sec.

Billy and his father are having an argument, and, for many, a typical scene follows with shouting, swearing and two people unable to understand each other. The point is that Billy lied to his dad about what he was spending his money on, as he knew that his dad would not like him learning ballet. There is nothing wrong with Billy dancing (that's where Billy's dad was at fault) but it was wrong for him to lie (that's where Billy was at fault).

Bible bit

Read **Luke 2:41-52.**

Short talk on how this story relates to life with parents who nag!

Group bit

Re-read the story in Luke 2:41-52.

- If there was one thing you could change about your parents, what would it be?

- If there was one thing your parents could change about you, what do you think it would be?

- Play the **listening challenge** (see page 12). Get people into pairs and have them sit with their backs to each other. Give out various simple line drawings to one of the pair and a blank sheet to the other. Explain that the one with the drawing must describe the pattern so that their partner can draw it – they must not look over their shoulder.

- How do you think Jesus' parents felt when they couldn't find him?

- How do you think Jesus felt when they didn't understand him?

- Do you think Jesus was wrong by not telling his parents where he was going?

- For those whose parents aren't Christians: do your parents give you a hard time for your faith? How does this make it hard when it comes to obedience?

- When do you think it is OK to go against what your parents say/ask? (Emphasise that we shouldn't do something our parents ask us to do that may hurt us.)

- Do you ever feel misunderstood by your parents?

- What does verse 51 say in the story? (Jesus went home and was obedient.)

- What can we learn from this story? (For example: sometimes our parents do get it wrong and they don't always understand us but they are still our parents and we do have to obey them.)

Pray to finish

Pray for any difficult family situations people are in now. Pray that we may learn how to communicate with our parents better and understand that they are only human!

Can you follow instructions?

A read-and-do test   **Time limit: 3 minutes**

1. Read all that follows before doing anything

2. Write your name in the upper right-hand corner of this page

3. Circle the word 'corner' in sentence two

4. Draw five small squares in the upper left-hand corner of this page

5. Put an X on each square

6. Put a circle around each square

7. Sign your name under line five

8. After your name write 'yes, yes, yes'

9. Put a circle around number 7

10. Put an X on the lower left-hand corner of this page

11. Draw a triangle around the X you have just made

12. Call out your first name when you get to this point

13. On the reverse side of this paper add 6950 and 9805

14. Put a circle around your answer

15. Now that you have finished reading carefully, do only numbers 1 and 2

Please be quiet and watch the others follow the instructions.

From Michael Puffett and Sheldon Rottler, *Red Hot Ice-Breakers*

The listening challenge

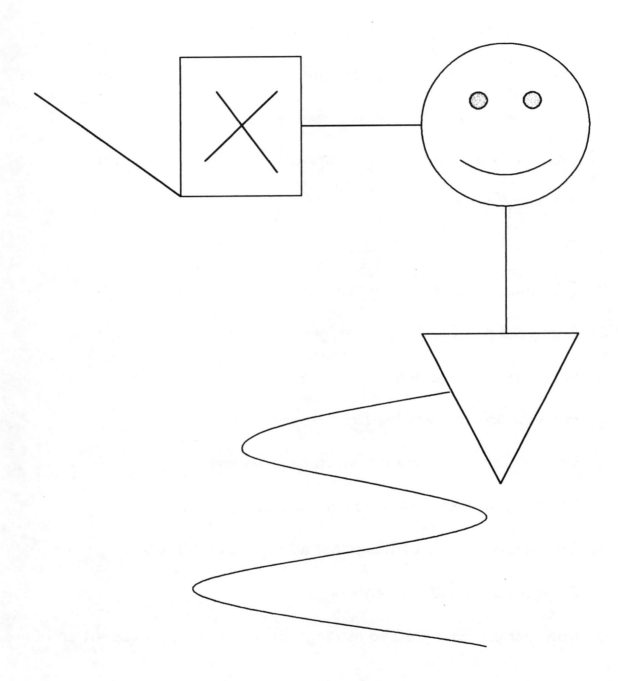

(This game can be done with any simple line drawing,
so why not have a few different ones at hand?)

Week 2
It's like I don't exist!

Icebreaker

• Lifeboat challenge

Get into groups and hand out the lifeboat challenge (see page 15) – they must work out who must stay on the boat and why. They need to share their final list and reasons with the rest of the groups. Ensure that there is a mix of ages and leaders within the groups.

• Mood sheet

Hand out the mood sheets (see page 16) and ask people to circle the face(s) that describes how they feel when they think about family. Then ask them to choose which face(s) describe how they feel when they are ignored or over-looked. Get into small groups and explain why they have chosen the different faces. Share recent times when they have felt ignored or overlooked.

The point is that we can feel as if we're not of any value in life or as if no one would notice if we didn't exist. But it's not like that with Jesus. He notices us, and he doesn't tell us to shut up or go away or ignore us – he welcomes us with open arms and he is glad we exist.

Video clip

Show a clip from *The Simpsons* episode 'Moany Lisa' where Lisa feels blue and that no one cares what she has to say or offer. The clip starts from beginning of episode and lasts for 12min 75sec.

The point is that so often it can feel as if even our own families don't have time for us, and it is easy to conclude that we might as well not exist!

Bible bit

Read Mark 10:13-16.

Short talk on how the young are especially important to Jesus.
Pick up on 1 Timothy 4:12.

Group bit

- Share stories of when you have felt you were being ignored.

- How does it feel to be ignored or talked over?

- Share stories of when people have said something out of anger and regretted it afterwards. (Perhaps when others have said something to make us feel worthless they also regretted it.)

- Get everyone to shut their eyes and listen as you read the poem 'My child' (see page 17).

- Reread the story in Mark 10:13-16.
  - Get people to picture themselves as one of these children and be part of the story.
  - How does it make you feel when the disciples turn you away?
  - How does it make you feel when Jesus calls you to him and takes you into his arms?
  - Do you want to be held by him?
  - What do you want to ask him or say to him?
  - Encourage people to write their thoughts down as prayers or pray together as a group.

Pray to finish

Pray that people may know that they are valuable and they are planned. It is not a mistake that they exist, and even when people make them feel like that, God would never do this. Pray that people may be open to being held by Jesus and believing his love and acceptance of them.

Lifeboat

An ocean liner sinks at sea and seven people escape in a lifeboat. Unfortunately, the lifeboat only has enough room and supplies for five people. Therefore, two people will have to abandon the lifeboat. The ocean contains hungry sharks, so the people who leave the boat will die.

You must select two people who will have to be sacrificed. Justify the reasons why you picked these two and also justify why the five should live.

To help you make your selection, the following information is presented:

1. A 1-year-old baby travelling with its grandmother. The baby is extremely sick, suffering from a rare disease, but possibly treatable.

2. The baby's 55-year-old grandmother. She is in good health but has been depressed since the death of her husband.

3. The captain of the ocean liner. He is 31 years old and has six children. His wife is dead and he has no insurance.

4. A 77-year-old scientist. He is one of the original developers of the atomic bomb which was dropped on Japan during the Second World War. His recent research might possibly lead to the cure for lung cancer in the next year or two.

5. A 42-year-old pregnant woman. Gossip on the ship indicates that she might be a prostitute. Her heavy make-up and style of clothing seem to indicate that the gossip is true.

6. A 21-year-old university student. He is a rugby player. He is extremely brilliant and has an IQ of 140. He is a homosexual and very active in gay rights.

7. A 72-year-old doctor who is a specialist in rare childhood diseases. Some people think that he is a saint, but what most of them do not know is that he is a drug addict. The police are investigating him because there is evidence that he sells drugs to young people.

From Michael Puffett and Sheldon Rottler, *Red Hot Ice-Breakers*

Mood sheet

How do you feel when you think about family?

How do you feel when you are overlooked or ignored?

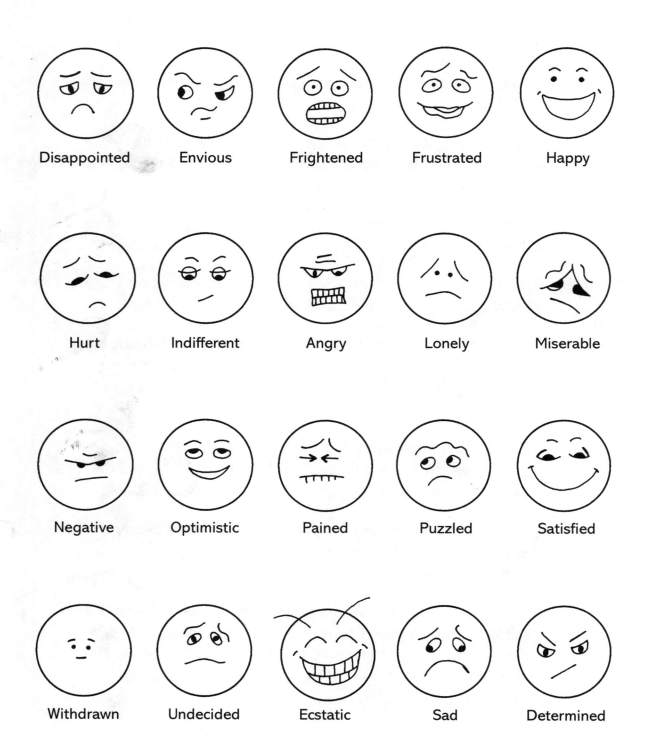

Disappointed	Envious	Frightened	Frustrated	Happy

Hurt	Indifferent	Angry	Lonely	Miserable

Negative	Optimistic	Pained	Puzzled	Satisfied

Withdrawn	Undecided	Ecstatic	Sad	Determined

My Child,

you may not know me, but I know everything about you.
I know when you sit down and when you rise up;
I am familiar with all your ways.
Even the very hairs on your head are numbered,
for you were made in my image.
In me you live and move and have your being,
for you are my offspring.
I knew you even before you were conceived;
I chose you when I planned creation.
You were not a mistake,
for all your days are written in my book.
I determined the exact time of your birth and where you would live;
you are fearfully and wonderfully made.
I knitted you together in your mother's womb,
and brought you forth on the day you were born.
I have been misrepresented by those who don't know me.
I am not distant and angry, but am the complete expression of love,
and it is my desire to lavish my love on you,
simply because you are my child and I am your Father.
I offer you more than your earthly father ever could,
for I am the perfect Father.
Every good gift you receive comes from my hand,
for I am your provider and I meet all your needs.
My plan for your future has always been filled with hope,
because I love you with an everlasting love.
My thoughts towards you are countless as the sands on the seashore,
and I rejoice over you with singing.
I will never stop doing good to you,
for you are my treasured possession.
I desire to establish you with all my heart and all my soul,
and I want to show you great and marvellous things.
If you seek me with all your heart you will find me.
Delight in me and I will give you the desires of your heart,
for it is I who gave you those desires.
I am able to do more for you than you could ever imagine,
for I am your greatest encourager.

I am also the Father who comforts you in all your troubles;
when you are broken-hearted I am close to you.
As a shepherd carries a lamb, I have carried you close to my heart.
One day I will wipe away every tear from your eyes,
and I'll take away all the pain you have suffered on this earth.
I am your Father and I love you even as I love my Son Jesus,
for in Jesus my love for you is revealed;
He is the exact representation of my being.
He came to demonstrate that I am for you and not against you,
and to tell you that I am not counting your sins.
Jesus died so that you and I could be reconciled;
his death was the ultimate expression of my love for you;
I gave up everything I love that I might gain your love.
If you receive the gift of my Son Jesus you will receive me,
and nothing will ever separate you from my love again.
Come home and I will throw the biggest party heaven has ever seen.
I have always been Father, and will always be Father.
My question is . . . Will you be my child?
I am waiting for you.

. . . Love
Your Dad
Almighty God

Week 3
Sunday Christian?

Icebreaker

• Chubby bunnies

Choose a couple of volunteers and have a bin at the ready! Ask the volunteers to put marshmallows in their mouth one by one and after each one to say, 'I am a Christian and I go to church.' The winner is the one who gets the most marshmallows in their mouth.

Play it a couple of times.
Alternatively, make up a game that illustrates the same point.

The point is that the more marshmallows they had in their mouths, the harder it was to speak. Often we go to church on Sunday but everything else we do and say during the rest of the week contradicts (goes against) what we say and do and believe on the Sunday. There is no such thing as a Sunday Christian – you are a Christian or you aren't.

Video clip

Show a clip from *The Mask* where the character discovers how different he can be when he has this mask on. The clip is 16min 45sec into the film and it runs for 90sec.

Explain that we may have different masks we wear – we may be one person on Sunday and another person at home and another person at school. The problem is Jesus can see through this mask and he wants us to take down our masks and be a Christian wherever we are. He wants us to live without contradictions (things that don't match up/go together).

Bible bit

Read John 2:13-22.

Short talk on how Jesus was so angry with these people who claimed to be holy yet they were behaving in an unholy way. Jesus does not like us only living for him and loving him when it is easy or when we are at church – he sees through our masks.

To illustrate this, project an OHP on to the wall/screen and have 'GOD' printed large on the acetate. Place various silhouettes of objects on the acetate (for example, a bottle, a boy/girl, a computer) – see how these silhouettes block the view of 'GOD'. It is the same in life – things sometimes get in the way.

Group bit

- Are there things you wouldn't say or do at church but wouldn't think twice about doing at home/school?
- Have you ever done something because your friends were – something that you didn't really want to do/say?
- Make a list of the things that get in the way of your relationship with God.
- What did the video clip say about masks? Is it true?
- What happened when Jim Carrey put on the mask? Is this similar to the 'masks' people put on in life?
- How do we remove our masks? Read James 1:7-8 out loud.
- What happens when we wear masks? How does it make you unstable?
- Do you need to remove a mask?
- Read the 'balloon man' story and application (see page 21).

Pray to finish

Pray for people to commit all their life to Jesus – not just Sundays. Pray for those who are finding it hard to live as a Christian at home/school.

Hand out balloons (filled with helium) and write on the balloons things people want to let go of. Go outside and release them as a visual way of letting go and taking down our masks.

The balloon man

Everywhere he went the man carried brightly coloured balloons. He enjoyed watching them float above his head. And it was easy to hold the string in his hand or wrap it around his wrist and take his colourful balloons wherever he went. The other people where he worked were accustomed to seeing them. They didn't mind; it brightened the office a little. Even at night the balloons would float above the man as he slept.

One day he went to the fair and had a great time. At the fair he could blend into the atmosphere of the rides and lights and noise. Oh, sometimes people tried to buy his balloons, thinking he was a vendor, but of course he wouldn't sell even one.

At one of the booths he filled in a ticket to see if he could win a free ocean cruise. He certainly didn't plan on winning, but it wouldn't hurt to try. Yet two weeks later a telegram came – he had won! He would enjoy great entertainment and the world's finest chef providing his meals. Talk about excited! The man started packing immediately. He was ready to go days before it was time to leave.

On the morning of the big day he called a taxi and had the driver take him to the dock slowly. He had to go slowly because the balloons wouldn't all fit in the taxi and he had to hold some of them out the window. At the dock he unloaded his luggage, went aboard ship, and was welcomed by the officials who had planned his trip. They even had someone take his suitcases down to his cabin while he stayed on deck and enjoyed the activity. The ship was crowded. Many people were aboard just to say goodbye to friends. Confetti, horns, streamers – and lots of balloons. He felt right at home.

Eventually the visitors left and the voyage was begun. It was great! Sailing on a big ocean liner was really refreshing. It also made him very hungry. Someone told the balloon man that the evening meal was in just one hour – a welcome relief!

When they rang the bell, he started to walk towards the dining room on the second deck. The aroma of the food was so enticing. There was one problem, though. Whoever had designed the ship hadn't left enough room for a man with a handful of balloons to get down the passageway. He could do it if he released some of the balloons, but the balloon man just couldn't do that. He had seen some crackers and cheese on the upper deck earlier, so he went back and ate that instead. It was good. Maybe not as good as the chef's dinner, but it was good enough. Besides, he had his balloons. That night the sunset was beautiful and it was exciting to walk along the deck. But it sure got cold quickly after that. Sea air not only made him hungry, it made him tired as well. He asked one of the ship's crew where his room was, and the crewman took him down a wide hall and opened the door of his cabin.

It was beautiful. They had given him one of the classiest rooms on the ship. He could see that the interior decorating was the best. And the bed looked inviting. Unfortunately, the door to the cabin was so designed that he couldn't get all the balloons in without breaking some. He tried, but it just wouldn't work.

Back on deck he found some blankets and a deck chair. He tied the balloons round his wrist and the arm of the chair and tried to sleep. The next morning he was still tired. All that day he ate crackers and cheese and that night he slept on the deck again.

The next morning the balloon man received an engraved invitation from the captain of the ship. He had been invited to sit at the captain's table and enjoy the speciality of the world-famous chef. He would prepare it especially for the balloon man. All that day the man watched as the crew made preparations for the evening banquet, and at 8pm the ship's bell rang and the passengers began to go to the dining room. The man watched them go. Soon he could hear the murmur of voices, the sound of silverware, and the clink of glasses. The aroma of the food became even more enticing.

He stood at the end of the passageway for some time. Finally he walked to the back of the ship. He could still hear the dinner in progress. He reached in his pocket and felt the engraved invitation. He knew there was a special place reserved for him at the captain's table. Then he looked up at his balloons. It was hard to do, but slowly – very, very slowly (he hadn't unclenched his hand for years) – one at a time he uncurled his fingers. One by one the balloons began to drift away.

As he watched, the wind caught them and blew them out of sight. The man turned and walked down the passageway. That night, as a guest at the captain's table, he enjoyed the finest meal and the best companionship he'd ever known.

From Wayne Rice, *More Hot Illustrations for Youth Talks*

Application

Are you hanging on to a handful of balloons that keep you from being close to Jesus?

What are the names of your balloons? Are they friends? Bad habits? Sex? Possessions? Your pride? Your popularity?

Maybe it's time to just let those balloons go so that you can enjoy the relationship with Christ that is yours for the taking.

'Let us throw off everything that hinders and the sin that so easily entangles us' (Hebrews 12:1).

Pray for people to let go of the different masks they put on and be proud to be a Christian and not hide it from others.

Week 4
What's the point in being nice?

Icebreaker

• Musical niceties

Sellotape a piece of paper to each person's back and hand out pens to everyone. Play some music and ask people to move around the room and write something nice about each person on the bit of paper on their back. Each person must write on every other person's back even if they do not know the person that well. (Leaders need to ensure this happens and to check that only nice things are being written!)

Give people time to read their slips of paper.

Discuss how it made them feel to read these things. Were they glad people were nice?

Video clip

Show two clips from the film *Pay it forward*. The first clip can be found 6min from the start of the film and it runs for 5min 30sec. This clip shows Kevin's first day of school and the assignment he is set to come up with an idea to change the world and to put it into action.

The second clip can be found 31min 16sec into the film and it runs for 2min. This clip shows Kevin's idea called 'Pay it forward'.

The film illustrates how, if we all do our bit, we can and will make a difference. In the film the 'Pay it forward' movement travels across the USA as people pay forward the good deeds done to them. Even if this didn't happen, it is still worth doing because if we all said there's no point in doing good, what would the world be like?

Bible bit

Read Luke 17:11-19.

Short talk on how Jesus healed these men not to be thanked but because they needed to be healed. We may not see the results of the good we do and we may not know whether others are grateful for our kindness but that doesn't make what we do pointless.

Share testimonies of when being nice felt pointless but later you discovered it was worth it.

Group bit

- Share stories of when someone did something for you and they didn't even know they had done it.

- Share stories of when you helped someone. Were they grateful? How did it make you feel when you helped them?

- Have you ever done something and thought it had no effect and then later discovered it had helped someone?

- Read 'Save the starfish' and application (see page 25).

- All choose a nice thing to do for someone that will cost you – it will take guts or time or even money – and do it this week. Being nice isn't always easy – look at the greatest act of love: what Jesus did for us by dying on the cross. It was far from easy but that one act means we can all be saved. Everyone writes down their act of kindness and they are all put together in an envelope – we will look at them in a couple of weeks and share what happened and how we felt.

- Discuss these sayings: 'One snowflake may melt on your cheek but enough snowflakes together can stop traffic' and 'You may be only one drop in the ocean but the ocean is made up of many drops.'

Pray to finish

Pray for people to see with God's perspective and see that they can do something to help change this world. Pray for people not to let fears or problems get in the way of helping people. Pray for the things people have decided to do this week to help someone.

Save the starfish

There was once a little boy who was walking along the beach and all of a sudden he came upon thousands of starfish that had washed up on the beach. The tide was going out, and for some strange reason the starfish ended up stuck on the beach. They were all doomed because they couldn't survive being out of the water in the hot sun until the next high tide. The little boy realised this and frantically started picking up starfish and throwing them, one at a time, back into the water.

A man who was walking along the beach saw the boy doing this and he yelled at the boy, 'Son, what in the world are you doing? Don't you know that there are thousands of starfish on this beach? And don't you know that this beach goes on for miles and miles? There is no way in the world you can save all those starfish!'

The little boy thought about that for a moment, then turned to the man, picked up a starfish and said, 'Yeah, I know. But I can save this one.' And he threw it as far as he could into the ocean.

From Wayne Rice, *More Hot Illustrations for Youth Talks*

Application

Sometimes we get discouraged because we can't solve all the problems of the world, or see all of our friends and family come to Christ, or do everything that we feel God wants us to do.

But we can do something. And something is always better than doing nothing at all. You aren't going to be able to win the whole world to Christ. But you can share the love of Jesus with one person. Scripture tells us that all of heaven rejoices when just one person is saved.

You can't do everything – but you can do a lot more than you think you can. And God will take what you do, bless it and multiply it – just like he did with a little boy's lunch beside the sea of Galilee.

So pick up a starfish and throw it. That's all God wants you to do. He'll do the rest.

Week 5
Bullying

Icebreaker

• Toilet teaser

Choose four people and take them out of the room. Explain to them that they are to go back into the room and act out something whilst sitting on a seat. They cannot say what they are doing but can use sounds. The others are trying to guess what they are doing. The choices are: riding a roller coaster; being tortured; watching a football match; riding a horse. Meanwhile, tell the rest of the group that the four people will be acting as if they are going to the toilet. Invite the four people back and begin. Once people have stopped laughing explain to these four what the others thought they were doing. Ask them how it felt to be laughed at and not know what others were thinking.

Video clip

From *Never been kissed* this clip shows news reporter, Josie, thinking back to her teenage years when she was bullied at school. She is about to go back to high school undercover to write a story for the paper and starts to panic.

The clip can be found 9min 53sec into the film and it runs for 3min 47sec.

The point is that many of us may relate to Josie's experience – either we were Josie or we were one of the people laughing at her or tormenting her. This clip shows Josie's pain and misery. We are going to look at what Jesus says about those others may pick out as different or 'easy targets' for bullying, and what he would do and with whom he would rather spend his time.

Bible bit

Read John 8:1-11.

Short talk on how Jesus accepts those whom others cast aside or mock or torment. In this passage we see how he draws the attention away from the woman by writing on the floor and so saves her from more embarrassment. Throughout the Gospels we see that Jesus chooses to spend his time with the poor, the ill and the outcasts, instead of the Pharisees. We should not make the mistake the Pharisees made by thinking we are better than others or putting others down to make ourselves feel or look better.

(This could pick up on Matthew 7:3-5.)

As an illustration of Christ's acceptance of us and our importance to him, do the '£5 sketch' (see page 28).

Group bit

- Have you ever been bullied? How did you feel?
- Have you ever been a bully? How did you feel?
- Have you ever gone along with your friends when they have bullied someone? How did you feel?
- Think of someone you know who doesn't fit in (it might be yourself). Should they change, or should society accept them as they are? Why do people see them as misfits? Has anyone taken the time to get to know them? Would you?
- Do you pay more attention to what God says about you or what people say about you?
- Why is it difficult to earn both the approval of people and of God?
- Think of someone who is ignored or laughed at in your school. What could you do to show them acceptance and love? Decide to speak to them or speak up for them this week.
- Read 'The puppy nobody wanted' (see page 29).

Pray to finish

Pray for people who feel worthless or have been made to feel this way. Pray for us to know our own value and the value of others, and not to make others feel like they are not valuable.

£5 Sketch

Do you want £5?

Start off by offering the £5.

I have a £5 note here and I will give it to anyone who wants it! I'm not joking, who would like this £5 note?

Wait for show of hands: I am going to give this £5 to one of you, but first, let me do this.

Proceed to crumple the note up.

Then ask: Who still wants it? It's a bit tatty but do you want it?

Wait for show of hands.

Well, what if I do this? **And drop it on the ground and start to grind it into the floor with your shoe.**

Pick it up, now crumpled and dirty. Now, who still wants it? My shoes are quite dirty but it's not too bad, anyone . . .?

Spit on the £5 note and ask: How about now? Any takers?

Wait to see if anyone still raises their hand. Begin to rip the note up and then ask: Surely no one still wants it now?

See if anyone does.

A £5 note is always worth £5 — even ripped up it is worth £5. You have all learned a very valuable lesson. No matter what I did to the money, you still wanted it because it did not decrease in value. If I creased it, trod on it, spat on it, and even ripped it, it is still worth £5. Many times in our lives, we are dropped, crumpled, and ground into the dirt by the decisions we make and the circumstances that come our way. We feel as if we are worthless. But no matter what has happened or what will happen, you will never lose your value. Dirty or clean, crumpled or finely creased, you are still priceless to those who love you. The worth of our lives comes not in what we do or who we know, but in who we *are*. You are special. Don't ever forget it. And remember that all those around us are also special so we must try not to make them feel crumpled. We must try to love them like Jesus loves them.

The puppy nobody wanted

The sign on the door said 'Puppies for sale' and so the little boy went inside to look. The man inside the pet shop showed him five little puppies who were ready now to leave their mother. They were about the cutest dogs the little boy had ever seen.

'How much are they?' the little boy asked.

The man replied, 'Some are fifty dollars, some are more.'

The little boy reached into his pocket and pulled out some change. After counting it, he said, 'I have a dollar and forty-seven cents.'

'Well, I'm afraid I can't sell you one of these puppies for a dollar and forty-seven cents, little boy. You'll have to save your money and come back next time we have more puppies for sale.'

About that time, the pet store owner's wife brought out another puppy that had been hidden in the back of the store. It was smaller than the other puppies, and had a bad leg. It couldn't stand up very well, and when it tried to walk, it limped very badly.

'What's wrong with that puppy?' asked the little boy. The pet store owner explained that the veterinarian had examined the puppy and had discovered it didn't have a hip socket. It would always limp and always be lame.

'Oh I wish I had the money to buy that puppy!' exclaimed the little boy with excitement. 'That's the puppy I would choose!'

'Well that puppy is not for sale, son. But if you really want him, I'll just give him to you. No charge.'

But the little boy got quite upset at this. He looked straight at the pet store owner and said, 'No, I don't want you to give him to me. That little dog is worth every bit as much as the other dogs you have for sale. I'll give you a dollar and forty-seven cents now, and I'll give you fifty cents a month until I have paid for this dog in full.'

The pet store owner was perplexed. 'You don't really want to spend your money on this little dog, son. He is never going to be able to run and play with you like the other puppies.'

Then the little boy reached down and rolled up his pant leg to reveal a badly twisted, crippled left leg, supported by a big metal brace. He looked up at the pet store owner and said, 'Mister, I don't run and play too good myself. I figure this little puppy is going to need someone like me who understands.'

From Wayne Rice, *More Hot Illustrations for Youth Talks*

Application

Scripture says that you were 'bought with a price'. Jesus paid a very high price for you when he went to the cross. He did it because he loves you and wants you to be with him. And he understands what you are going through. As it says in the book of Isaiah, he was the 'Suffering

Servant' who 'bore our iniquities'. He took all of the pain we deserve upon himself.

You may feel like an outcast, a nobody. You may think nobody likes you, that nobody wants you. You may be suffering, going through difficult times. Though all of that, you can be sure Jesus understands. He knows exactly how you feel.

Week 6
When life gets stormy

Icebreaker

• Get a parachute and find a large space or go outside and play different parachute games. All sit round the edges and shake the parachute. Have a ball and put it on the parachute – half the group must try to shake the ball into the hole in the middle and the other half must try to shake the ball away from the hole in the middle. Invent some other games.

Video clip

This clip from *Forces of nature* shows the natural disasters that take control and stop Ben getting to his own wedding. Ben and Sarah face rain, storms, hurricanes and fire.

The clip can be located 1hr 23min 40sec into the film and it runs for 2min 17sec.

The point is that we can never fully be in control; there is always a higher power at work. Another good illustration is from *The Simpsons* where Maggie appears to be driving the car but then we see it is a toy car wheel and Marge is really in the driver's seat. As Christians we also need to let go and let God.

Bible bit

Read Mark 4:35-41.

Short talk on what we build our lives on and how Jesus said if we have our foundations built on him, even when life gets stormy we will not fall down.

Expand on these sayings: 'Sometimes God calms the storm, sometimes he calms his child' and 'Lord, help me remember that nothing is going to happen today that you and I together can't handle.'

Group bit

- Each write down on a piece of paper the storms in your life at the moment. Fold the pieces of paper up and put them in a pile by a cross as a way of giving these things back to God.

- Share stories of when you felt out of control.

- Read this poem called 'Let go and let God':

As children bring their broken toys,
with tears for us to mend,
I brought my broken dreams to God,
because he is my friend.
But then instead of leaving him in peace
to work alone,
I hung around and tried to help,
with ways that were my own.
At last, I snatched them back again and cried,
'How can you be so slow?'
'My child,' he said, 'what could I do?
You never did let go.'

Author unknown

- Share stories of when you were too stubborn to let someone help you and you ended up making a mess of what you were doing.

Pray to finish

Pray for people's 'storms' or the problems they are going through now. Pray that we may be able to trust God with everything and not try and fix things without him. Pray that we may trust God to look after us and not give us more than we can handle. Pray for God to either calm the storms (sort out the problems) or calm his children.

Week 7
Pop-idol wannabe?

Icebreaker

• Guess that star!

Have some large A4 posters of various pop stars or film stars and cover them up with sections of paper. Reveal the posters bit by bit and get the young people to guess who they are. You could divide them into teams and have prizes for those who guess the most.

Go round and say which famous person you admire the most and why.

The point is that we all have people we admire or idolise, and many of us want to be famous. There is nothing wrong with this but if fame or the idea of fame goes to our heads too much, then it can be dangerous.

Video clip

Show the clip from *Notting Hill* – nearly 43min into the film for 1min 30sec – where Julia Roberts talks about how fleeting fame is.

The point is that the grass is always greener! There is nothing wrong with being famous or with wanting to be (God can use us), but we shouldn't think this is the ultimate success and place to get to in life.

Bible bit

Read John 13:1-17.

Short talk on how Jesus, the Son of God, was famous but still humble – he even washed his disciples' feet. Talk about serving others.

Get the leaders to wash the young people's feet as a sign of humility.

Group bit

• Who/what did you want to be when you were younger?

• If you could be any famous person, who would it be and why?

- Would you like to be famous? Why or why not?

- Think of some famous people – do they have any problems?

- Read James 1:10-11. What does God say happens to beauty and fortune? Why do we pursue these things, then? What should we pursue instead?

- How should we use fame and fortune if we receive it?

- Read 'Make me like Joe' and application (see page 35).

- Who would you like to be like? Why?

- Who would you notice was missing first if they died: your bin man or your doctor?

- How can you serve your friends and family and even your enemies?

- Discuss ways of serving people you know or your community, and decide to do it as individuals or a group.

Pray to finish

Pray that whether we are famous or not in the future, or popular now or not, we may remain humble and still do as Jesus did – serve others. Pray that we may never think so much of ourselves that we are not able to serve others less fortunate.

Make me like Joe

A drunk was miraculously converted at a mission. Prior to his conversion, Joe had gained a reputation of being a dirty wino for whom there was no hope, only a miserable existence in the ghetto. But following his conversion to a new life with God, everything changed. Joe became the most caring person that anyone associated with the mission had ever known. Joe spent his days and nights hanging out at the mission doing whatever needed to be done. There was never any task that was too lowly for Joe to take on. There was never anything that he was asked to do that he considered beneath him. Whether it was cleaning up the vomit left by some violently sick alcoholic or scrubbing the toilets after careless men left the bathroom filthy, Joe did what was asked with a soft smile on his face and with a seeming gratitude for the chance to help. He could be counted on to feed feeble men who wandered into the mission off the street, and to undress and tuck into bed men who were too out of it to take care of themselves.

One evening, when the director of the mission was delivering his evening evangelistic message to the usual crowd of still and sullen men with drooped heads, there was one man who looked up, came down the aisle to the altar and knelt to pray, crying out for God to help him to change. The repentant drunk kept shouting, 'O God, make me like Joe! Make me like Joe! Make me like Joe! Make me like Joe!'

The director of the mission leaned over and said to the man, 'Son, I think it would be better if you prayed, "Make me like Jesus!"'

The man looked up at the director with a quizzical expression on his face and asked, 'Is he like Joe?'

From Wayne Rice, *More Hot Illustrations for Youth Talks*

Application

The first real communication of anything spiritual usually comes through people who demonstrate loving humility in the regular turn of daily events and especially in the rough spots of life. When we share the humble spirit of Christ in the workplace, at school, at home, or wherever we are, we do more to point people to Christ than any kind of preaching or evangelistic technique. Our goal is to let people see Jesus in us, to be a reflection of him.

Someone has said, 'You may be the only Jesus a person ever sees.' What would that person see in us? Let us be an accurate reflection of Jesus, who 'being in very nature God, did not consider equality with God something to be grasped, but made himself nothing, taking the very nature of a servant' (Philippians 2:6-7).

Week 8
But I like it here!

Icebreaker

- Relay race

Divide people into four groups. Set up a starting line and a finishing line in a large open area. Name one group 'babies' and tell them they can only get around by moving on their bottoms. Name the next group 'toddlers' and tell them they can only crawl. The next group are 'children' and they can walk. The last group are 'adults' and they can run. Have a relay race within these groups.

Explain to people that the babies and toddlers were extremely restricted in the race and the children were quite limited. Link the race to the Christian life and introduce the idea that we need to grow in our faith and not stay as 'baby' Christians or else we restrict God's influence in our lives.

Video clip

This clip from *Chicken Run* shows Ginger trying to convince the other chickens not to settle for their life of captivity but to take risks for a better life. The clip can be found 16min 30sec from the start and it runs for 1min 30sec.

Many people spend their lives striving for safety and comfort. Christians don't have this luxury. God calls us to make hard decisions, leave our comfort zones, and step out in faith, believing that he is leading us to a better place where he will fulfil his promises.

Bible bit

Read Matthew 14:22-32.

Short talk on how we need to step out of the boat. It is easy to judge Peter for losing faith, taking his eyes off Jesus and therefore sinking, but what about the others? – they didn't even step out of the boat!

Talk about faith being spelt R-I-S-K.

Pick up on the saying: 'You may be on the right track but you'll get knocked over if you are standing still.'

Group bit

- When or where do you feel safe?

- As a child did you have a security blanket or favourite toy that you took everywhere?

- Do you remember, as a child, being resistant to toilet training or other changes that meant you had to do more for yourself?

- Read 'Great babies' and application (see page 38).

- In your Christian life, in what ways do you think you need to change or grow (for example, pray more, read the Bible more, trust God more, learn more, tell others about God more)?

- What things in your life make up your comfort zone?

- What is the craziest thing you've felt God told you to do? What happened? Did you go through with it?

- Read Genesis 12:1-5. How much information did God give Abram about where he was going and what would happen? Could you pack up and leave like Abram did? Why or why not?

Pray to finish

Pray that we may not settle where we are or think we have made it as a Christian. Pray that we may be obedient to Jesus' call to 'Come' towards him and step out of our comfort zones. Pray for particular things people want to grow in.

Great babies

A group of tourists were travelling through Europe visiting historical sites. They were impressed that so many small villages were the birthplaces of great artists, poets, composers and political leaders.

 While the group was strolling through a particularly picturesque village, one of the tourists approached a man who was sitting in front of a building and asked, 'Excuse me, but were any great men or women born in this village?'

 The old man thought for a moment and replied, 'No. Only great babies!'

From Wayne Rice, *More Hot Illustrations for Youth Talks*

Application

Everyone starts off as a baby – with the opportunity to grow into greatness. This is true not only in the world but also in the kingdom of God. When we become Christians, we are 'born again' as 'babies in Christ'. We have to grow.

 Paul wrote, 'Brothers, I could not address you as spiritual but as worldly – mere infants in Christ. I gave you milk, not solid food, for you were not yet ready for it. Indeed, you are still not ready' (1 Corinthians 3:2). These words were written to adult believers, yet Paul addressed them as 'infants'.

 But we can't stay babies for ever. We need to grow. The writer to the Hebrews said, 'Therefore let us leave the elementary teachings about Christ and go on to maturity . . .' (Hebrews 6:1). That's why it's important to be in worship services, Sunday school, youth group, Bible studies and the like. They are opportunities for growth. The 'great men and women' of the faith, just like you, started out as babies.

Week 9
Hopeless?

Icebreaker

- Play 'Dreams can come true' by Gabrielle.

- Hand out sheets of paper and ask the young people to draw or write a dream of theirs – for now or the future.

- Encourage people to share what they have done and explain it to the rest of the group.

Video clip

This clip from *Sister Act 2* shows Rita give in to apathy and how Deloris helps her realise her dream. The choir is a great success and proves everyone who doubted them wrong. The clip can be found 50min from the beginning and it runs for 11min 50sec.

It is easy to have our dreams deflated by the negative attitudes or comments of those around us, but as Christians we have hope for the future and for now – we have God on our side and he can do anything with or through us, and so we must not be afraid to dream big!

Bible bit

Talk about Jesus' death and resurrection as the reason why we can have hope. Pick up on verses such as Jeremiah 29:11 and Romans 12:2 to talk about the future and not being held back because of the attitudes of society and those around us.

Group bit

- When you were younger what did you want to be when you were older?

- What do you dream about doing or being in 10 years' time?

- Has God ever given you a dream to do for him? Has it happened yet? How will you make it happen?

- If you could do anything what would it be?

- What attitudes of the area/culture you live in get in the way or tell you different?

- Read Ephesians 3:20. Does this encourage you?

- Read 'Not-so-identical twins' and application (see page 41).

Pray to finish

Pray for people's dreams and hopes – that they may be realised. Pray for revelation of hope in apathetic people. Pray for the local area and schools. It may be a good idea to pray individually for people and ask for God to give people dreams if they don't have any.

Not-so-identical twins

There were once two brothers who were identical twins. Now even though they looked exactly alike, they were exact opposites when it came to their personalities. One brother was an eternal optimist – he always saw good in everything and everybody. The other brother, however, was an eternal pessimist – he never saw good in anything anywhere.

One Christmas their parents decided to try an experiment on them to see if there was any way that the two brothers could find some balance in their personalities. To the pessimist son the parents gave a bright, shiny bicycle. To their optimist son they gave a bag filled with nothing but straw. They put the presents under the tree with the boys' names on them and waited to see what would happen.

On Christmas morning the two boys ran downstairs to discover what they had received from their parents. Upon finding the bicycle, the pessimist proclaimed, 'A bike? Why did you give me a bike? It's too cold to ride outside, and, besides, I will probably fall and hurt myself. I can't believe you got me a lousy bike!'

The optimist opened his present, found the bag of straw and thought for a minute. Suddenly he ran to the back yard and began looking around frantically. His parents and brother were completely puzzled, and they finally asked him, 'What in the world are you doing?' To which he replied, 'Well, after getting that bag of straw, I just know there's a pony around here someplace! I just haven't found him yet!'

From Wayne Rice, *More Hot Illustrations for Youth Talks*

Application

Attitude can make a huge difference in your circumstances. When things happen to you at home, at school, with your friends, you have two choices: you can take the high road or the low road. The high road is to remain positive and look for the good in your situation. The low road is to be negative and to see only the bad. One road leads to happiness, the other to despair. Really, the choice is yours. Circumstances don't have to control your life. You can instead control how those circumstances affect you. You have the power.

As Christians, we have every reason to take the high road and to be optimistic about life. Because of Christ, we have hope – real hope. We know that no matter what happens, God is in control and we have the victory that Christ won for us on the cross. The apostle Paul was in prison when he wrote, 'Rejoice in the Lord always. I will say it again: Rejoice!' (Philippians 4:4). That's the kind of attitude we need to have.

Week 10
Hold your tongue!

Icebreaker

- Taboo

Play the board game 'Taboo' with the whole group divided into two teams. The teams take it in turns to nominate one person to pick a game card and try and explain a word to their team without using the word or any of the other words on the card. If the team guesses correctly without using taboo words they gain a point. If a taboo word is used no point is gained and the next team take their turn. Each turn is timed. Maybe have a prize for the winning team.

The point is that it can be really hard not to say the things we know we shouldn't.

Video clip

This clip from *The Lion King* is 1hr 14min from the start and it runs for 2min 15sec. The clip is where Scar confronts Simba and reminds him of his guilty past. These words are very hurtful and almost stall Simba from claiming his rightful throne.

Words may not be true (like in this clip – Simba did not kill his father but he was made to believe he did) but they are very powerful and can disguise the truth.

This clip shows that the saying 'Sticks and stones may break my bones but words can never hurt me' is often very far from the truth.

Bible bit

Read Matthew 12:33-37.

Short talk on how what is in our hearts will overflow into our lives and our conversations. Perhaps pick up on influences in our lives that may not help our speech – violent/offensive music and films, for example.

Read James 3:3-12.

Talk about the contradiction in praising God one minute and then swearing or being nasty in what we say.

Group bit

- Share stories of people's words hurting you.

- Read Proverbs 16:28. When has gossip harmed you, or your gossip harmed others?

- Read Proverbs 10:19. Why is this good advice?

- Have you lost a friend or damaged a friendship because of something you said or gossip you believed?

- Take the 'My words' cards (see page 44) and think about the things you say that you know you shouldn't. Make your own taboo card by writing these on the card. It might be swearing or taking God's name in vain, or lying or gossiping or being nasty about your friends or your enemies. You might like to keep this card in your wallet to remind yourself of your decision.

- How might we deal with our friends gossiping or being nasty about people? Come up with some practical ideas. For example, walk away, stand up and make people see the power of their words, or add something positive about the person.

Pray to finish

Pray that people may be able to stick to their decisions on what they won't say any more. Pray for God's strength and insight into what damage our words could do. Pray that as Christians we may be able to set an example in what we say as well as what we do. Thank God that he can use us to bless each other in what we say and what we don't say.

MY WORDS . . .

_____

_____

_____

_____

_____

_____

_____

_____

_____

Also available by Suzi Stock

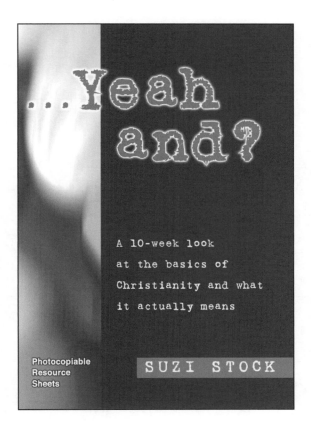

...Yeah and?

A 10-week look
at the basics of
Christianity and what
it actually means

Photocopiable
Resource
Sheets

SUZI STOCK

. . . Yeah, and?

a ten-week look at the basics of Christianity for young people

1500593
1 84417 079 9

...Yeah, and? contains 10 weekly sessions for young
people, each designed to last about 40 minutes.
Each session includes group discussion, activities,
scripture, personal testimony and prayer.

Photocopiable take-home sheets enable the young
people to supplement their reading with activities
which include questions, thoughts, facts and verses.
To conclude, there is an outline programme for a
weekend away together which can be used at the
end of the course.